So You Think

BERKHAMSTED

A QUIZ & MISCELLANY

THE FRANCIS FRITH COLLECTION

www.francisfrith.co.uk

First published in the United Kingdom in 2005 by The Francis Frith Collection®

Hardback edition published in 2005 ISBN 1-84589-225-9

British Library Cataloguing in Publication Data

So You Think You Know? Berkhamsted
Text adapted from original material supplied by Berkhamsted Local History and Museum Society, with particular contribution from Jennifer and Jimmie Honour

The Francis Frith Collection
Frith's Barn, Teffont,
Salisbury, Wiltshire SP3 5QP
Tel: +44 (0) 1722 716 376
Email: info@francisfrith.co.uk
www.francisfrith.co.uk

Printed and bound in England

Front Cover: **BERKHAMSTED, TOWN HALL c1910** ZZZ04935t
(Berkhamsted Local History and Museum Society)

The colour-tinting is for illustrative purposes only, and is not intended to be historically accurate

2005 photographs by Ken Wallis

Aerial photographs reproduced under licence from Simmons Aerofilms Limited.

The publisher gratefully acknowledges the assistance of Berkhamsted Local History and Museum Society and the Dacorum Heritage Trust in providing additional illustrative material for this book.

Every attempt has been made to contact copyright holders of illustrative material.
We will be happy to give full acknowledgement in future editions for any items not credited.
Any information should be directed to The Francis Frith Collection.

AS WITH ANY HISTORICAL DATABASE, THE FRANCIS FRITH ARCHIVE IS CONSTANTLY BEING CORRECTED AND IMPROVED, AND THE PUBLISHERS WOULD WELCOME INFORMATION ON OMISSIONS OR INACCURACIES

CONTENTS

2 Berkhamsted Miscellany

28 Berkhamsted Quiz Questions

54 Berkhamsted Quiz Answers

58 General History Quiz Questions

82 General History Quiz Answers

86 Francis Frith - Pioneer Victorian Photographer

BERKHAMSTED, THE SCHOOL CHAPEL ZZZ04910 (Berkhamsted Local History and Museum Society)

BERKHAMSTED MISCELLANY

One of the best-known traders in Berkhamsted in the early 19th century dealt in ironwork. James Wood produced a range of ironware, including candle-snuffers, rat-traps, skewers, meat safes, fireguards and sieves. The firm still trades in the town today, but now focuses on a nursery and giftware business.

Until very recently, Peter Latchford produced Frithsden wines from his vineyard in the nearby village of Frithsden. Furthermore, on the southern slopes of the town, on the Sunnyside Allotments, grapes are still grown today.

The coat of arms (with its 13 gold balls) of Richard, Earl of Cornwall, younger brother of Henry III, is incorporated in Berkhamsted's coat of arms; it can be seen on the wooden post in the High Street outside the Civic Centre.

When the Black Prince left Berkhamsted to fight at the battles of Poitiers and Crécy he took with him archers from Berkhamsted and nearby, including Stephen Champneys, Edward le Bourne, Richard of Gaddesden, and Henry of Berkhamsted. Berkhamsted archers practised shooting in butts near the town centre on what is now called Butts Meadow.

St John's Well was a spring which appears in medieval records, and was still in the 19th century reputed to cure sore eyes, a 'holy well.' The water ran down St John's Well Lane to the river until it dried up in the mid 20th century.

A court of 'pied poudreux' (old French for 'dusty feet') was held during fairs to give speedy justice while the dust of the fairground was still falling from the feet of pedlars and others involved in disputes.

A number of roads in Berkhamsted are named after Ashridge and the families associated with the house through the centuries. These include Bridgewater Road, Egerton Road, Brownlow Road, Ellesmere Road, Belton Road, and Ashridge Rise.

The Duke of Cornwall, afterwards Charles I, came to Berkhamsted in 1616. 20 horsemen met him at Brickhill Green and escorted him down Chesham Road and Castle Street, where he stopped to hear a speech of welcome in Latin by 'one of the Schollers of the free Schole.' He then proceeded to Berkhamsted Place, where he hunted in the park. It was not until the 20th century that a Duke of Cornwall was to visit Berkhamsted School again.

BERKHAMSTED, HALSEY'S COTTAGE, CASTLE STREET c1890 ZZZ04929 (C H Sills)

BERKHAMSTED, HIGH STREET AND THE BAPTIST CHURCH c1955 B407001

An entry in the churchwarden's accounts for 1660 reads: 'The happy yeare of King Charles the Seconds restauration to his government'. Church bells rang and fireworks were let off. The parish spent 10s on a 'barrell of beare' for the celebrations and 15s 2d on powder and match. The bellringers received £1.

There are three coats of arms above the door of the former Bourne School, that of Thomas Bourne, that of the town, and that of General Finch.

Tucked away on the southern edge of the common is Moor Cottage, built in 1774 by the Berkhamsted Vestry as the Pest House for the isolation of those with smallpox and other infectious diseases. Now a private house, an inscription inside bears witness to its earlier use.

Peter the Wild Boy once strayed as far as Norfolk, so Mr Fenn had a leather collar made for him with a brass ring bearing the inscription: 'Peter, the Wild Man from Hanover. Whoever will bring him to Mr Fenn at Berkhamsted, Hertfordshire, shall be paid for their trouble.' This collar still exists and is preserved at Berkhamsted Collegiate School.

BERKHAMSTED, DEAN INCENT'S HOUSE c1955 B407043

In Victorian times and in the first half of the 20th century many a Sunday School treat started with a trip by horse-drawn canal boat from Castle Street to Newground; the children then continued on foot or by wagonette to the Bridgewater monument above Aldbury for a picnic.

While the railway was being built a steam locomotive, the 'Harvey Coombe', was brought by canal to Bourne End. A temporary track was laid to transport truckloads of soil from the Northchurch tunnel and the Billet Lane cutting to build the embankment between Bourne End and Boxmoor. Henry Weatherburn, its driver, sometimes gave local residents a free ride before the railway was officially opened.

Those who heed the notice 'Freshly picked plums for sale' and drive up the steep lane to Broadway Orchard every summer are buying plums from one of the remaining fruit orchards of Lane's Nurseries.

Sibdon Place is named after the little hamlet of Sibdon Castle, close to Clunbury in Shropshire. William Cooper's grandparents, Thomas and Ann Cooper, were married there in 1784. Their eldest son William and his wife Sarah lived in Clunbury, where William Cooper of sheep dip fame was born in 1813. William Cooper's invention of sheep dip, which was made in Berkhamsted, was to take the name of the town all over the world.

BERKHAMSTED, THE TOWN HALL 2005 ZZZ04962 (Ken Wallis)

BERKHAMSTED, THE INNS OF COURT MEMORIAL, THE COMMON 2005 ZZZ04957 (Ken Wallis)

One of the pupils at the Girls' School at the turn of the century was Clementine Hozier, who later became Lady Churchill. She lived for several years with her mother and sisters in the High Street close to Rectory Lane.

Mr William Fisher, who lived to be over 90, worked for Messrs Wood at the time of the 19th-century enclosure of Berkhamsted Common, and recalled the events as an old man. He helped to erect the fencing, 'and sometime afterwards I was detailed off to clear away the twisted remains of the fences.' He recounts vividly the return of the navvies who helped with the work to Berkhamsted Station, where they were paid for their night's work.

Flint gathered from the demolition of some of the interior dividing walls during the 19th-century restoration of St Peter's was stored in Matthew's builders' yard and later used for the building of Sunnyside Church.

The firm of Penny & Thorne, solicitors, still practises in the town in the same premises as in Victorian times at 175 High Street.

The part of the park used for exercises by the Inns of Court during the First World War became known as Kitchener's Field. On the Common, old trenches dug out at this time are still visible.

In 1917 the Court Theatre opened in Berkhamsted to provide films, plays and musicals for the troops stationed in the town. It closed in 1960 and was converted for use by Tesco. Following a fire in 1969, the present supermarket was built.

One of the first performances of 'Peter Pan' took place at Egerton House, staged especially for the Llewellyn Davies children, one of whom was ill. When Egerton House was under threat of demolition, help was sought from the author, James Barrie, but he was too old and infirm to help.

BERKHAMSTED, ASHLYNS SCHOOL c1955 B407042

BERKHAMSTED, ST PETER'S CHURCH c1960 B407044

When the Ashlyns estate was purchased by the London Foundling Hospital, the governers were required by the Land Registry to place 20 boundary posts round the estate. These were a copy of the posts in London, with the carving of a lamb. Several still remain today, including one in Hilltop Road and one near Velvet Lawn.

During the Second World War the actor Derek Fowlds came with his mother and sister from London to live with his grandmother in Ellesmere Road. He attended Chapel Street Infants' School, Victoria School and Ashlyns School.

In medieval times, parks were places where deer were kept for hunting and the raising of venison. They were used also to produce timber and for grazing livestock. Berkhamsted Park was probably created in the 12th century.

BERKHAMSTED, HIGH STREET c1955 B407035

BERKHAMSTED, THE GIRLS' GRAMMAR SCHOOL AT THE BOURNE SCHOOL ZZZ04932
(Berkhamsted Local History and Museum Society)

After the Court Theatre closed, Berkhamsted Amateur Dramatic and Operatic Society performed in the Kings Hall and the Civic Centre. In 1970 the Society staged 'A Day in the Death of Joe Egg', with nine-year old Sarah Brightman playing the part of Joe as a child. Sarah's mother was an active member of the society for many years; her father built a number of houses in the town in the 1970s and 1980s. Sarah went on to West End fame, notably in 'The Phantom of the Opera'.

Egerton-Rothesay School came about from the merger of two private schools: Rothesay School, founded in the High Street in 1922, later in Shrublands Road, and Egerton School, founded in 1950 in Charles Street. The schools merged in 1984 and opened a senior department when the Thomas Bourne School building became vacant. The new school was opened in September 1988 by the Prime Minister, Mrs Thatcher.

The wool and cloth industry was a major part of medieval Berkhamsted's economy. In the reign of Richard II there was a subsidy of four pence per broadcloth. Every piece was inspected by the alnager, an official who examined the cloth. If the cloth was up to standard, he gave it his seal. It was illegal to sell unsealed cloth.

Francis Egerton, 3rd Duke of Bridgewater, the 'Canal Duke', is buried in Little Gaddesden Church with the epitaph: 'Memorable among those who were honoured in their generation and were the glory of their times.' A better-known memorial to him is the Bridgewater Monument, from the top of which are extensive views of the surrounding countryside.

When Berkhamsted Place was built in the 16th century, stone was used from the ruined castle. When Berkhamsted Place was demolished in 1967 many worked stones from the castle, possibly from the chapel, were found.

Gorseside, a house used as the sales office for Castle Village, has been confirmed by thermographic imaging to be 17th-century. Originally a farmhouse, it has additions of the 18th, 19th and 20th century, and is thus typical of a house that has been altered through the centuries to the needs of its occupants.

Polly Page, born in 1787, was the daughter of the innkeeper of the King's Arms. Louis XVIII, while living in exile at Hartwell House, Aylesbury, always changed horses at the King's Arms, and usually contrived to see 'Pretty Polly'. Later Polly became innkeeper at the death of her father, and she received Queen Victoria and the Prince Consort when they changed horses there.

A large number of halfpenny lace tokens have been found bearing the words 'Pay at Leighton, Berkhamsted or London'. This indicates that Berkhamsted was an important centre of the lace trade in the 18th century.

BERKHAMSTED,
JOHN RAVEN'S BRASS,
ST PETER'S CHURCH ZZZ04899
(Berkhamsted Local History and Museum Society)

BERKHAMSTED, GRAND UNION CANAL c1960 B407049

In 1932 East & Sons of Gossoms End won a contract to make 202 lock gates for the Grand Union Canal. The timber yard finally closed in the early 1990s, and the Stag Lane area was developed as a light industrial estate.

Thomas Squire, a Quaker, who lived at The Homestead, experimented with seeds and cuttings. On 26 July 1841 he planted out a small apple tree, after having cheered Queen Victoria and the Prince Consort as they drove through the town. The tree did well, and Thomas called the tree the Victoria and Albert. Lane's Nurseries marketed the apple as 'Britain's latest apple' and renamed it Lane's Prince Albert.

Building the Tring summit, which had to carry the canal to 405 feet above sea level, involved digging a cutting over 1½ miles long and over 30 feet deep in places.

William Cooper used arsenic and sulphur to manufacture his powdered sheep dip. The sulphur was dressed by means of a machine called the 'Joggler', invented by George Dean. At first this was operated by hand, but later it was driven by an old mare.

BERKHAMSTED, THE COURT HOUSE AND THE PARISH CHURCH c1960 B407052

The school chapel at Berkhamsted School was dedicated in June 1895 and was designed by Mr C H Rew, a Berkhamsted architect. The design was inspired by the Venetian church of Santa Maria dei Miracoli. It is a fitting memorial to the achievements of the headmaster, Dr Fry, later Dean of Lincoln.

The St Peter's Parish Magazine of December 1878 reported that the Managers of the National Schools had decided to increase the fees except for the 'labouring poor', on a scale up to 9d, which was about the amount that the maintenance of each child at the school cost.

John Tawell, who lived at the Red House, was hanged in Aylesbury Market Place in 1845 for the murder of his former mistress. He was the first murderer to be caught as a result of a message transmitted by the electric telegraph.

In 1906 the gas works moved to Billet Lane. Here an old horse called Ruby was later used to haul coal in small wagons along a single rail track. Part of the track can still be seen today.

In 1855 the Rev John Wolstenholme Cobb, of St Peter's, gave two lectures on 'The History and Antiquities of Berkhamsted' to the Mechanics' Institute. These lectures were later printed in book form. The book has been reprinted a number of times, and is still available today.

BERKHAMSTED, TUDOR HOUSE, BACK LANE (NOW CHURCH LANE) ZZZ04940
(Berkhamsted Local History and Museum Society)

BERKHAMSTED, SUNNYSIDE ALLOTMENTS 2005 ZZZ04963 (Ken Wallis)

Adelbert, Earl Brownlow, and his wife, Adelaide, Lady Brownlow, were the last private owners of Ashridge. She was a great hostess and noted for her hospitality, which brought royalty and many distinguished visitors to Ashridge. Lady Brownlow died in 1917 and Lord Brownlow in 1921.

In the 1932-33 football season, a 17-year old Berkhamsted lad, Frank Broome, scored 53 goals. In 1934 he turned professional with Aston Villa. He played regularly in the First Division, and in 1946 he transferred to Derby County. He won seven England caps.

BERKHAMSTED, THE SATURDAY MARKET 2005 ZZZ04968 (Ken Wallis)

During the First World War, Lord Brownlow placed his estate at the disposal of the Inns of Court Officer Training Corps, which was billeted in the area. His waiting room at the station became the Quartermaster's office and stores, and part of Ashridge House became a military hospital.

In 1983 the Town Hall Trust converted the ground floor into a shopping arcade called Lamb's Shops, which was formally opened by Lord Bernard Miles on 31 December 1983. Trade flourished throughout the 1980s, but changing patterns of retail trading led to the Trust entering into a 25-year lease with City Centre Restaurants, and most of the ground floor was converted into a Caffé Uno.

BERKHAMSTED, THE CANAL 2005 ZZZ04967 (Ken Wallis)

When the new Foundling Hospital was built in Berkhamsted, many things from the previous hospital in London were incorporated in it. The staircase from the former girls' wing was installed; the original light pedestals were placed along the drive; the statue of Thomas Coram was re-erected on a new base; and the older stained glass windows from the London chapel were installed in the new chapel, and more recent ones in the concert hall. The memorials to governors and secretaries were placed in the crypt, together with the remains of Thomas Coram and a bust of Handel. Handel's organ was installed in the new chapel.

The first cinema in Berkhamsted was the Gem, a corrugated iron hut in Cowper Road, specially adapted in 1910. Before this films had been shown in the Town Hall and by a travelling show in the meadow by the Crooked Billet.

The castle witnessed several fine historical pageants in the 20th century. The first was in 1922, 700 years after the building of St Peter's Church; it was written by the eminent historian, G M Trevelyan, who lived in Kings Road, Berkhamsted.

BERKHAMSTED, THE RIVER BULBOURNE, MILL STREET 2005 ZZZ04946 (Ken Wallis)

BERKHAMSTED QUIZ QUESTIONS

1. The original Berkhamsted School in Castle Street was founded by Dean Incent. In what year was this?

2. What was the name of the architect who designed the Town Hall, and in what year was it opened?

3. Where was the Tudor Market House, and what happened to it?

4. Berkhamsted Castle is a motte and bailey design. What was a motte, and what purpose did it serve?

5. For what use was Ashlyns School originally built?

6. A notorious murderer lived in Berkhamsted in Victorian times. Who was he, whom did he murder and what was his fate?

7. What connection did Geoffrey Chaucer have with Berkhamsted?

8. One of the most famous people connected with Berkhamsted was William of Normandy. Which event in Berkhamsted involving William was of great historical importance?

9. Thomas à Becket is best remembered for his martyrdom in Canterbury Cathedral, but what was his connection with Berkhamsted?

10. Which famous Prince of Wales spent his honeymoon at the castle?

BERKHAMSTED, THE FORMER CANAL-SIDE LOWER MILL WHARF 2005 ZZZ04952 (Ken Wallis)

BERKHAMSTED, THE TOWN HALL c1910 ZZZ04935 (Berkhamsted Local History and Museum Society)

11. The King's Arms displays the coat of arms of which monarch?

12. Which public house in Berkhamsted is unique in having its front entrance facing the canal?

13. The Swan, originally an inn on the corner of Chesham Road, brewed its own beer in the 19th century.
Who kept the inn at the time?

14. The HSBC bank building stands on the site of an earlier inn. What was its name?

15. Farmers from the Midlands and Wales driving their cattle and sheep to London would rest their animals in enclosures during their long journey. Which inn in Berkhamsted particularly welcomed them?

BERKHAMSTED, THE COURTHOUSE, BACK LANE AND THE WAR MEMORIAL 2005 ZZZ04960 (Ken Wallis)

16. Berkhamsted still had two watermills in 1900. Where were they?

17. William Cooper arrived in the town in the early 1840s and became world famous for his manufactured products. What did he produce?

18. The second gas works was sited off Billet Lane and ceased to operate when natural gas pipes were laid. The first works was much closer to the town centre. Where was it?

19. Locke and Smith had a site off Water Lane before the First World War. What was their trade?

20. Henry Lane was a nurseryman and founded a business in Berkhamsted in 1777, later exporting grapevines to France and Germany. He produced a famous apple variety. What was it called and why?

BERKHAMSTED, THE CANAL AND LOCK c1965 B407108

BERKHAMSTED, THE KING'S ARMS ZZZ04922 (Berkhamsted Local History and Museum Society)

21. When was Berkhamsted Castle last occupied?

22. What was the Collegiate School in Castle Street first called?

23. Berkhamsted had two workhouse sites. Where were they?

24. The Court Theatre stood on the corner of Water Lane and Back Lane (Church Lane). Why was it called The Court?

25. General de Gaulle could be seen in Berkhamsted during the Second World War.
Why was this?

26. The Quaker Meeting House was built in 1818.
    Is it still standing?

27. There are parish churches in Northchurch and Berkhamsted.
    Which one is the oldest?

BERKHAMSTED, THE CASTLE IN THE TIME OF EDWARD IV ZZZ04900
(Berkhamsted Local History and Museum Society)

BERKHAMSTED, HIGH STREET AND THE PARISH CHURCH c1955 B407003

28. An event brought the Wesleyan Methodists to Berkhamsted. What was that?

29. The Church of the Sacred Heart in Park Street was built in 1967, replacing the earlier Roman Catholic Church. Where was it?

30. The first Baptist Chapel was built in 1722 nearer the town centre. Where was it?

BERKHAMSTED, ASHRIDGE COLLEGE c1965 B407095

31. Indications of the site of the first railway station are still visible, but where?

BERKHAMSTED, THE TOTEM POLE 2005 ZZZ04950 (Ken Wallis)

32. The railway reached Berkhamsted in 1837. Who advised on the route? Who built it? Who operated it?

33. As well as several coachbuilders, Berkhamsted had a motorcycle manufacturer. Who was he, and where was his workshop?

34. The High Street was a turnpike road in the 18th century. What was the name of the turnpike trust? When was it formed? Where was the nearest tollgate?

35. Commercial traffic on the canal declined from the middle of the 20th century. When was the canal classified as a 'recreational cruiseway'?

36. Old photographs and documents refer to Graball Row. Where was it and why was it so called?

37. Sainsbury's had a shop in the High Street before the days of self-service. The premises remain, but where?

38. 173 High Street, previously Figgs the Chemist, has very old timbers. From which century do they date?

39. Mrs Bishop and her daughter Mrs Halsey lived in an old cottage in Castle Street where they sold chitterlings and other savoury dishes. What were chitterlings?

40. What is the purpose of the monument at the top of New Road on Berkhamsted Common?

41. There is an impressive monument to Mary Smith-Dorrien in Berkhamsted. Where is it located?

BERKHAMSTED, THE PLAQUE ON SAYER'S ALMSHOUSES 2005 ZZZ04947 (Ken Wallis)

BERKHAMSTED, THE TOWN HALL AND THE MARKET 2005 ZZZ04969 (Ken Wallis)

42. The war memorial outside the west door of St Peter's Church was moved there in 1952. Where was its original site?

43. Thomas Read's grave can be found in Chapel Street. Who was he?

44. A brass to John Raven can be seen in St Peter's Church. Who was John Raven?

45. John Sayer, chief cook to Charles II, lived at Berkhamsted Place. In his will he left money for the building of almshouses. Where would you find his tomb?

BERKHAMSTED, THE COMMON AND THE FORMER PARK 2005 ZZZ04956 (Ken Wallis)

46. Grim's Ditch or Grim's Dyke can be seen in the area. What is it thought to have been?

BERKHAMSTED, HIGH STREET c1955 B407013

BERKHAMSTED, DEAN INCENT'S HOUSE 2005 ZZZ04964 (Ken Wallis)

47. What is a totem pole doing by the canal bridge in Castle Street?

48. The original granite railway sleepers were replaced by timber and then concrete ones. Where can granite sleepers still be seen in the town?

BERKHAMSTED, THE SCHOOL, THE SCHOOL HOUSE c1960 B407047

49. The Bourne Gutter is reputed to flow with water at certain times. At which times, and where is it?

50. What was locally known as the Crown and Sausages?

BERKHAMSTED, MONK'S GARDEN, ASHRIDGE COLLEGE c1960 B407066

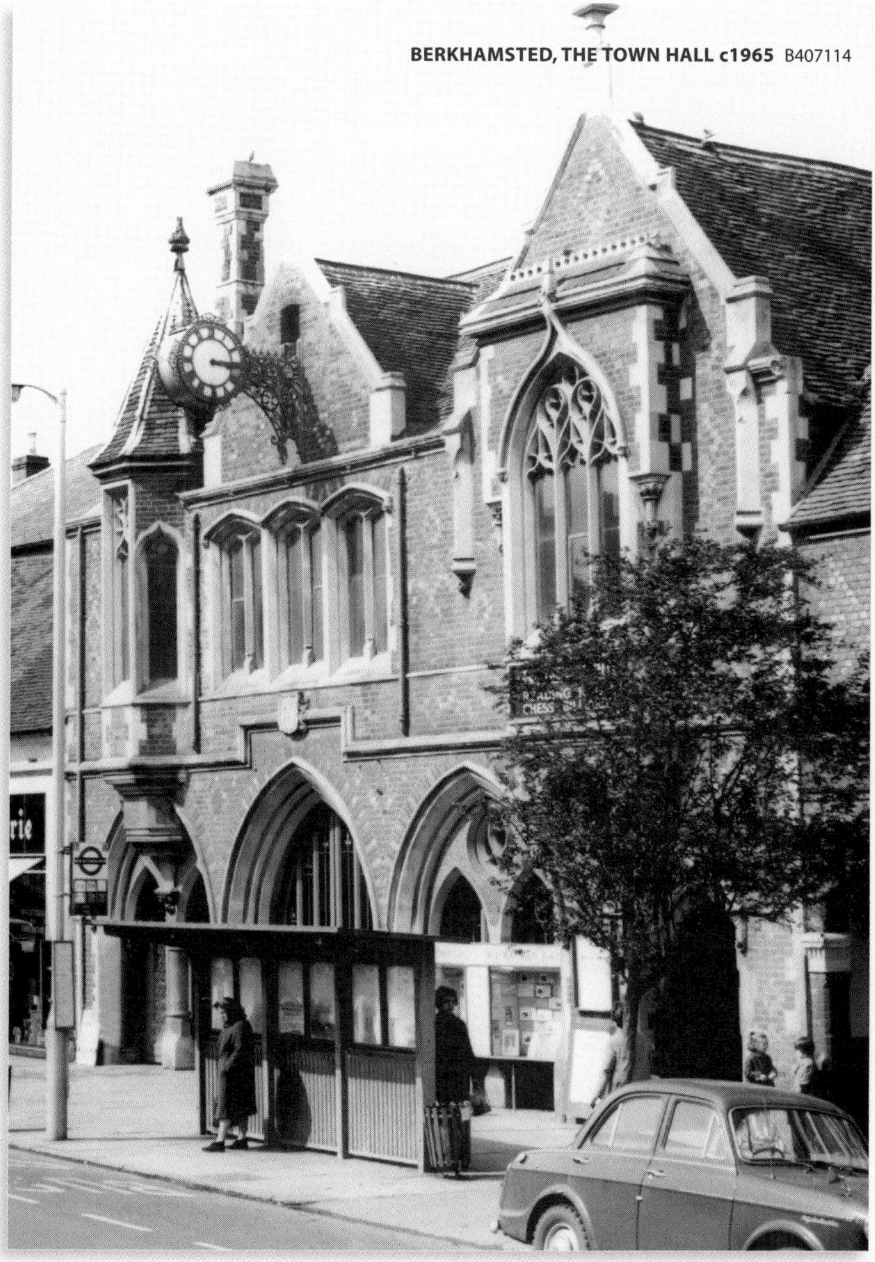

BERKHAMSTED, THE TOWN HALL c1965 B407114

BERKHAMSTED QUIZ ANSWERS

1. A licence was granted from the King in 1541. The first building was completed in 1544.
2. Edward Buckton Lamb. The Town Hall's opening ceremony was performed in August 1860.
3. It stood in front of Aitchisons, opposite the King's Arms. It was destroyed by fire in August 1854.
4. A motte was a man-made hill usually topped by a tower to be used as a last defensive position.
5. Captain Thomas Coram's Foundling Hospital, founded in London in 1740, moved to new purpose-built premises in Berkhamsted in 1935.
6. John Tawell poisoned his mistress, Sarah Hart, near Slough. He later moved to Berkhamsted where he lived in the Red House and married Sarah Cutforth. He was arrested in London and hanged in Aylesbury in 1845.
7. Geoffrey Chaucer, author of 'The Canterbury Tales', was Clerk of the Works at the castle.
8. After the defeat of King Harold in 1066 William marched on London and was met by Saxon noblemen at Berkhamsted. They swore allegiance to him and offered him the crown.
9. Thomas à Becket, later Archbishop of Canterbury, held the castle as Chancellor from 1155 to 1165.
10. In 1361 Edward, the Black Prince, married Joan, the Fair Maid of Kent, and they spent their honeymoon in Berkhamsted.
11. The arms of Queen Anne, 1702-1714.
12. The Rising Sun has its main entrance from the canal towpath.
13. The Foster family. They had a second maltings in Chapel Street, and supplied a number of other taverns as well as the Swan.
14. The Red Lion. The yard at the side of the bank is still referred to as Red Lion Yard.

15. The Goat. The nearby Three Close Lane had three enclosures for cattle and sheep.
16. The Upper Mill was in Mill Street beyond the Collegiate Music School. One of the millstones can still be seen there. Lower Mill was behind the Old Mill Hotel on the corner of London Road and Bank Mill Lane.
17. William Cooper invented a sheep dip in powder form combining sulphur and arsenic, which was used by farmers all over the world.
18. The three gasholders were sited in the Wilderness, now part of the Water Lane car park.
19. They were the largest firm of brewers in Berkhamsted and were later taken over by Benskins of Watford.
20. The apple was Lane's Prince Albert, originally called the Victoria and Albert, to commemorate the visit of Queen Victoria and the Prince Consort to Berkhamsted on 26 July 1841 on their way from Windsor to Woburn.
21. The castle was last occupied by Cicely, Duchess of York, who died in 1495.
22. The school was first known as 'Dean Incent's Free Schole and Chauntry in Berkhamsted'.
23. The first thatched workhouse was on the east corner of Park View Road and the High Street. The replacement was built in 1834 on the west corner of Kitsbury Road and the High Street.
24. The Court Theatre was named after the Inns of Court Officers' Training Corps, which was encamped in Berkhamsted during the First World War.
25. General de Gaulle lived for a while in Rodinghead, a house on the edge of the Ashridge Estate.
26. It is still in use, set back from the High Street between Boxwell Road and Kitsbury Road.

BERKHAMSTED QUIZ ANSWERS

27. St Mary's Northchurch has some Saxon walls, whereas St Peter's was built in 1222, possibly on the site of an earlier church.
28. The first Wesleyan Methodists arrived in 1837 with the railway construction workers.
29. The earlier Roman Catholic church, built in 1909, was in Park View Road. General de Gaulle worshipped there during the middle years of the Second World War. The building still survives.
30. It was in Water Lane and remained in use until the present chapel on the corner of Ravens Lane was built in 1864.
31. Evidence of the original pedestrian tunnel entrance can be seen adjacent to the bridge by the Crystal Palace public house.
32. George and Robert Stephenson advised on the route. The firm of W and L Cubitt built it. The line was operated by the London & Birmingham Railway Company until July 1846.
33. C E Southey & Co were car repairers and also assembled their own make of motorcycle in the early 20th century, using premises in Elm Grove. They also had a showroom on the corner of the High Street.
34. The Sparrows Herne Turnpike Trust was formed in 1762 to maintain a 27-mile stretch of roadway from Bushey Heath to the outskirts of Aylesbury. The nearest tollgate was at Newground on the Tring Road.
35. Several hard winters in the early 1960s hastened the decline in freight traffic and in 1968 the canal was classified as a 'recreational cruiseway'.
36. Graball Row refers to the shops between St Peter's Church and Water Lane on the north side of the High Street. It is so called because the stalls in the medieval market place were converted into permanent buildings.
37. Sainsbury's occupied premises at 230 High Street and was still in business in the 1970s. It had separate counters on either side of

the shop running from front to back, and specially-designed floor and wall tiles.

38. The 13th century. This is the oldest urban timber building in the country, and is thought to be part of a medieval hall house. It is not known when it was first used as a shop.
39. Chitterlings are the intestines of pigs or other animals prepared as a dish.
40. It was erected in memory of the 2,000 Inns of Court officers who trained in Berkhamsted and were killed during the First World War.
41. In the churchyard of St Peter's Church, Castle Street.
42. It was first erected on the wide pavement in the High Street near to Water Lane.
43. Thomas Read was a founder member of the Mechanics' Institute and took an active part in local affairs. The clock on the Town Hall was erected in his memory in 1897.
44. He was squire to the Black Prince.
45. The impressive marble-topped tomb can be found in the Lady Chapel of St Peter's Church.
46. Grim's Ditch or Dyke on the south of the town is possibly Bronze Age, and Grim's Ditch on the north of the town is probably Iron Age. They are thought to be defensive ditches, possibly marking boundaries between tribal territories.
47. It stands on the site of the former timber yard of J Alsford, and was commissioned by the firm. It was carved out of red cedar by Henry Hunt of the Kwakiutl tribe in British Columbia.
48. A few can be seen on the pavement near St Peter's Church. Others can be seen along the canal.
49. Legend has it that it only flows in time of war or when there is rumour of war. It is more likely that it flows when there is heavy prolonged rainfall. It flows past Bottom Farm on to Bourne End.
50. The King Edward VI public house, now demolished, in Mill Street.

GOUDHURST, MEASURING THE HOPS 1904 52571

GENERAL HISTORY QUIZ QUESTIONS

1. Which 20th-century Prime Minister was a proficient bricklayer and a member of the union?

2. In Victorian times, what powerful substance did many fashionable society ladies use to spice up their afternoon tea parties?

3. What was the first battle of the English Civil War on 23 October 1642?

4. Who was Queen Victoria's first Prime Minister?

5. Which Michigan-born dentist was arrested in Canada for the murder of his wife in London?

6. For what crime was Titus Oates pilloried in the stocks and flogged every year?

7. What crime was committed by Burke and Hare?

8. What language was Elizabeth I not fluent in? German, French, Latin, or Italian?

9. In 1834 six Dorset farm labourers were transported to Australia. By what name are these men usually known?

HORNING, ON THE BROADS 1902 48108

MARKET DRAYTON, MARKET DAY 1911 63338

10. At which battle was Richard III slain?

11. Who was the first Prime Minister to live at Chequers?

12. Who was the leader of the Women's Social and Political Union?

13. In which year were women granted the vote on the Isle of Man? 1881, 1902, 1912, or 1946?

RHYL, DONKEYS ON THE SANDS 1891 29151

14. Which king signed the Magna Carta in 1215 at Runnymede?

15. In which city was the infamous Peterloo Massacre on 16 August 1819?

16. Who were the mother and father of Elizabeth I?

17. Before the French Revolution in 1789, who is reported to have said 'Let them eat cake'?

18. Who wore two shirts in which to be executed, and why?

SHANKLIN, THE STAGECOACHES 1913 66211A

NEWQUAY, THE HARBOUR 1894 33522

19. Which queen was known as Bloody Mary?

20. Who was the only English pope?

21. Which British king married May of Teck?

22. At the outbreak of World War I, who was the British Prime Minister?

23. What great structure, designed by Joseph Paxton, was built in 1851?

24. What were the names of the two princes believed to have been murdered in the Tower of London in 1483?

25. What unusual accident eventually caused the death of the Prince of Wales, eldest son of George II?

26. Which of Dickens's novels depicts the struggles and strife of factory workers in Victorian England?

EVERSLEY, THE WHITE HART 1906 57011

CASTLETON, SPEEDWELL CAVERN 1909 61785

27. How old was William Shakespeare when he got married? 24, 25, 19, or 18?

28. What crime occurred on 8 August 1963 that shocked public opinion in Britain?

29. Who had to hide in an oak tree to save his life after a military defeat?

30. After Henry VIII's Dissolution of the Monasteries, what are some of the new owners of the monastery buildings rumoured to have done with some of the illuminated manuscripts they found?

KING'S LYNN, HIGH STREET 1908 60023

BOURNEMOUTH, INVALID'S WALK 1900 45226

31. In July 1888, 1,500 female employees went on strike at a factory at Bow in East London. What did they manufacture?

32. Who was the Irish saint who legend says saw the Loch Ness Monster in Scotland?
St Columba, St Patrick, St Andrew, or St Aidan?

33. Which English woman made this prophecy:
'Carriages without horses shall go, And accidents fill the world with woe. Around the world thoughts shall fly, In the twinkling of an eye.'?

34. Which tax was levied between 1696 and 1851?

35. How long did the Hundred Years' War last? 116 years, 94 years, 100 years, or 108 years?

36. Who was called the 'Old Pretender'?

37. In 1629 William Harvey published the details of a discovery he had made. What was it?

38. Put these wars and battles in the order in which they took place:
A. The Battle of Agincourt
B. The Battle of Hastings
C. Marston Moor
D. Wars of the Roses

39. In British army slang, what was a 'dead man'?

40. When was the Poll Tax first introduced in England?

SAFFRON WALDEN, FRY'S GARDEN 1907 58821

CLOVELLY, POST OFFICE, TRANSFER OF MAIL 1936 87551

41. Who was the first Prime Minister of Britain?

42. What is pannage?

43. What were the Welshmen of the Rebecca Riots, who dressed up as women, protesting against?

44. How many people did the 1715 Riot Act have to be read to, in order for them to be guilty of a felony, and liable to the punishment of death? 6, 12, 27, or 250?

CHALFORD, THE VILLAGE 1910 62713

45. What was the joint stock company, the South Sea Company, set up in 1711 to trade in?

46. In the Middle Ages, a split stick was used by royal officials to record sums of money paid. Notches were cut on it representing payments. What was it called?

EASTBOURNE, THE PIER 1925 77946

WEYMOUTH, THE SANDS 1909 61597

47. When did the Union Jack achieve its present pattern?

48. In 1752, September 2 was followed by September 14. What was the name of the new calendar system that involved this adjustment?

NEWBY BRIDGE, THE SWAN HOTEL 1914 67414

49. Coffee houses were patronised by literary giants such as Dryden, Johnson, and Pope. How many coffee houses were there in London in the 18th century?
10, 50, 250, or 1800?

50. Who was the first British Prime Minister to live at 10 Downing Street?

TENBY 1890 28091

GENERAL HISTORY QUIZ ANSWERS

1. Winston Churchill.
2. Opium.
3. Edgehill.
4. Lord Melbourne.
5. Dr Crippen. He buried her body in the basement of his London house.
6. For giving false evidence against Catholics.
7. They murdered people and sold their corpses to unscrupulous surgeons for dissection.
8. German.
9. The Tolpuddle Martyrs.
10. The Battle of Bosworth Field.
11. Lloyd George.
12. Emmeline Pankhurst.
13. 1881.
14. King John.

15. Manchester.

16. Henry VIII and Anne Boleyn.

17. Marie Antoinette.

18. Charles I. The weather was cold and he did not want to be seen shivering.

19. Mary I, the daughter of Henry VIII and Catherine of Aragon. She married Philip II of Spain, and was a devout Catholic. She earned her nickname from her persecution of Protestants.

20. Adrian IV, born Nicholas Brakespeare in 1100.

21. George V (she was known in this country as Mary).

22. Herbert Asquith.

23. The Crystal Palace.

24. Edward V and his brother Richard Duke of York, the sons of Edward IV.

25. He was hit on the head by a cricket ball.

26. 'Hard Times', published in 1854.

27. 18.

GENERAL HISTORY QUIZ ANSWERS

28. The Great Train Robbery.

29. Charles II.

30. They used them as lavatory paper.

31. Matches. They worked at the Bryant and May factory.

32. St Columba, born cAD521.

33. Mother Shipton, born in Norfolk in 1485.

34. Window Tax, which was payable on a house with more than six windows.

35. 116 years, between 1337 and 1453.

36. James III (the son of James II). In 1715 he gathered together a force of 10,000 men and invaded England. The Jacobites fought their way as far as Preston, where they were dispersed.

37. The circulation of the blood. He was physician extraordinary to James I.

38. B (1066) A (1415) D (1455-85) C (1644).

39. An empty bottle.

40. In 1222, on every person over the age of 14.

41. Robert Walpole. As first Lord of the Treasury between 1721 and 1742 he presided over the cabinet.

42. The right of tenants to graze their swine in the woods of a manor.

43. They destroyed turnpike houses, being unhappy about the levels of tolls.

44. 12.

45. Slaves in Latin America.

46. A tally.

47. In 1801, when the cross of St Patrick was added to the crosses of St George and St Andrew.

48. The Gregorian Calendar.

49. 1800.

50. Sir Robert Walpole (1676-1745).

FRANCIS FRITH

PIONEER VICTORIAN PHOTOGRAPHER

Francis Frith, founder of the world-famous photographic archive, was a complex and multi-talented man. A devout Quaker and a highly successful Victorian businessman, he was philosophical by nature and pioneering in outlook. By 1855 he had already established a wholesale grocery business in Liverpool, and sold it for the astonishing sum of £200,000, which is the equivalent today of over £15,000,000. Now in his thirties, and captivated by the new science of photography, Frith set out on a series of pioneering journeys up the Nile and to the Near East.

INTRIGUE AND EXPLORATION

He was the first photographer to venture beyond the sixth cataract of the Nile. Africa was still the mysterious 'Dark Continent', and Stanley and Livingstone's historic meeting was a decade into the future. The conditions for picture taking confound belief. He laboured for hours in his wicker dark-room in the sweltering heat of the desert, while the volatile chemicals fizzed dangerously in their trays. Back in London he exhibited his photographs and was 'rapturously cheered' by members of the Royal Society. His reputation as a photographer was made overnight.

VENTURE OF A LIFE-TIME

By the 1870s the railways had threaded their way across the country, and Bank Holidays and half-day Saturdays had been made obligatory by Act of Parliament. All of a sudden the working man and his family were able to enjoy days out, take holidays, and see a little more of the world.

With typical business acumen, Francis Frith foresaw that these new tourists would enjoy having souvenirs to commemorate their days out. For the next thirty years he travelled the country by train and by pony and trap, producing fine photographs of seaside resorts and beauty spots that were keenly bought by millions of Victorians. These prints were painstakingly pasted into family albums and pored over during the dark nights of winter, rekindling precious memories of summer excursions. Frith's studio was soon supplying retail shops all over the country, and by 1890 F Frith & Co had become the greatest specialist photographic publishing company in the world, with over 2,000 sales outlets, and pioneered the picture postcard.

FRANCIS FRITH'S LEGACY

Francis Frith had died in 1898 at his villa in Cannes, his great project still growing. By 1970 the archive he created contained over a third of a million pictures showing 7,000 British towns and villages.

Frith's legacy to us today is of immense significance and value, for the magnificent archive of evocative photographs he created provides a unique record of change in the cities, towns and villages throughout Britain over a century and more. Frith and his fellow studio photographers revisited locations many times down the years to update their views, compiling for us an enthralling and colourful pageant of British life and character.

We are fortunate that Frith was dedicated to recording the minutiae of everyday life. For it is this sheer wealth of visual data, the painstaking chronicle of changes in dress, transport, street layouts, buildings, housing and landscape that captivates us so much today, offering us a powerful link with the past and with the lives of our ancestors.

Computers have now made it possible for Frith's many thousands of images to be accessed almost instantly. The archive offers every one of us an opportunity to examine the places where we and our families have lived and worked down the years. Its images, depicting our shared past, are now bringing pleasure and enlightenment to millions around the world a century and more after his death.

For further information visit: www.francisfrith.co.uk

FRITH PRODUCTS & SERVICES

Francis Frith would doubtless be pleased to know that the pioneering publishing venture he started in 1860 still continues today. Over a hundred and forty years later, The Francis Frith Collection continues in the same innovative tradition and is now one of the foremost publishers of vintage photographs in the world. Some of the current activities include:

INTERIOR DECORATION

Today Frith's photographs can be seen framed and as giant wall murals in thousands of pubs, restaurants, hotels, banks, retail stores and other public buildings throughout the country. In every case they enhance the unique local atmosphere of the places they depict and provide reminders of gentler days in an increasingly busy and frenetic world.

PRODUCT PROMOTIONS

Frith products are used by many major companies to promote the sales of their own products or to reinforce their own history and heritage. Frith promotions have been used by Hovis bread, Courage beers, Scots Porage Oats, Colman's mustard, Cadbury's foods, Mellow Birds coffee, Dunhill pipe tobacco, Guinness, and Bulmer's Cider.

GENEALOGY AND FAMILY HISTORY

As the interest in family history and roots grows world-wide, more and more people are turning to Frith's photographs of Great Britain for images of the towns, villages and streets where their ancestors lived; and, of course, photographs of the churches and chapels where their ancestors were christened, married and buried are an essential part of every genealogy tree and family album.

FRITH PRODUCTS

All Frith photographs are available Framed or just as Mounted Prints and Posters (size 23 x 16 inches). These may be ordered from the address below. From time to time other products - Address Books, Calendars, Table Mats, etc - are available.

THE INTERNET

Already one hundred thousand Frith photographs can be viewed and purchased on the internet through the Frith websites and a myriad of partner sites.

For more detailed information on Frith companies and products, look at these sites:

www.francisfrith.co.uk

www.francisfrith.com

(for North American Visitors)

See the complete list of Frith Books at:

www.francisfrith.co.uk

This web site is regularly updated with the latest list of publications from The Francis Frith Collection. If you wish to buy books relating to another part of the country that your local bookshop does not stock, you may purchase on-line.

For further information, trade, or author enquiries please contact us at the address below:

The Francis Frith Collection, Frith's Barn, Teffont,
Salisbury, Wiltshire, England SP3 5QP.
Tel: +44 (0)1722 716 376 Fax: +44 (0)1722 716 881
e-mail: sales@francisfrith.co.uk

See all Frith products on the internet at www.francisfrith.co.uk